Candle, Thread, and Flute

POETRY BY KATHRYN HINDS

Luna Station Press

•

New Jersey

First Edition May 2013
ISBN: 978-1-938697-20-3

Cover Design & Layout:
Jennifer Lyn Parsons

Luna Station Press
576 Valley Road #197
Wayne, NJ 07470
lunastationpress@gmail.com

www.lunastationpress.com

Candle, Thread, and Flute

Acknowledgments

Many of the poems in this volume (some of them subsequently revised or retitled) have previously appeared in journals, magazines, and anthologies:

"In the Circle" and "Under This Warming Sun" were in *The Lyric*.

"Call to the Darkness" was in *Hudson Valley Echoes* and *SageWoman*.

"'If We Don't Turn the Wheel, It Will Not Turn'" was in *Hole in the Stone* and *SageWoman*.

"Invitation" was in *Tides* and *SageWoman*.

"A Dream I Had While Nursing My Son on Thanksgiving Morning," "Snow Leopard, Bronx Zoo," "To Bast," "To Deborah on the First Day of Spring," and "To My Love Asleep" were in *SageWoman*.

"Girl in Red," "Her Horse," "Rite of Spring," "The Shore," and "Spider" were in *The Red Queen*.

"Meeting" was in *Enchanté*.

"To the Cauldron Tender" was in *Harvest*.

"Sacrament" was in *Tides* and *Hole in the Stone*.

"Priestess Song" was in *Circle Network News*.

"Beltane," "The Corn," "The Last Night of November," "Spring Equinox," "Summerland," and "Winter Seed" were in *Hole in the Stone*.

"Late-January Roses" was in *The Garland Green*.

"Sunset Over Lake Ontario" was in *Stonepile Anthology 2*.

"Pomegranate" was in *Dead, Mad, or a Poet*.

My deepest thanks to the editors of these publications for their support and encouragement.

—KH

FOR ARTHUR

Contents

MASKS AND VOICES

TURNINGS

WATER AND OTHER ELEMENTS

Part One

MASKS AND VOICES

This too is an experience of the soul,
The dismembered world that once was the whole god

—Kathleen Raine
"Isis Wanderer"

GIRL IN RED

Oh, see my beautiful cloak,
my new red cloak—
how it blossoms roselike around me,
how my striding floats it behind me,
how in my stillness it spills
to my feet on the forest path.

Then with the hood pulled up
I am something else
in the deep, private dark:
a nameless babe in the womb,
or a silent, creeping, secret beast.

I throw my head back and howl—
surprise!

But there is no more skipping on the way—
something is changing,
shadows sliding away from the path;
the trees are massing,
the breeze is low, sharp
pungent with the scent
of hidden life, animal,
from caves and holes.

I want to go into a cave.
I want to be swallowed whole.
To know what they know—
the devourers.

Here I am!
Here I am!

Snow Leopard, Bronx Zoo

My daughters, born here, play
at stalking, chasing, mock attacks
on twitching tails, pausing now
to nuzzle deep my tolerant belly.
We are on display, and humans stand
to gawk at us, and shout and mimic
feline speech, devoid of sense.
Their emotions clear the bars with ease,
and none of them feel fear, although
I have paws the size of small
human heads, and teeth their fingers' length.

My daughters bound over unnatural boulders
to the tops of unnatural crags
whose mitigated steepness assures survival,
whose artifice conceals the cage doors—
we are blasphemously kept inside at night.
I rise to pace, with falseness underfoot,
as the keeper arrives with dead meat,
unpungent flesh of birds that never graced
my tameless mountains....
Dear Gods! If only I could hunt!
To smell the essence in the wind,
to cock the ear for clues,
to make myself invisible until the final rushing moment—
the blood and broken neck, the earned feast!

My daughters cannot learn this joy.
Unwary mouthfuls seldom come

within the bars. But on the other side,
small, well-fatted humans point and bare
their teeth at me. I taste my teeth,
contract and expand like thunder.
There is no answering flight—the bars
halt me, and my prey stares. I settle
my eyes on it all the while I consume
what the keeper has brought.
Imagination feeds me.

To Bast

You know the cat that waits in me,
restless by the door, to be let
out into the moonlight, patience
turning to a rising wail that
calls you to open for me. I
will hurtle to your garden

and shake my sistrum, Cat Face,
open my eyes to reflect
light in the darkness. My feet
are graceful; I am movement's
mistress when I feel you near,
and nothing lives that escapes
my senses. Then let me

into the dance of your furred
and whiskered kin, let me drop
the veil from my wildness, let
me know joy in the night and
in the morning be at peace
with the disgorged, gentled sun.

Sky Goddess

I arch my back in counterpoint
and overhead you arch
Lady of Heaven
your indigo body spangled with the suns
of all the worlds
My lover moves beneath me
and I gaze on him again
as if I am seeing the Earth
as it rises and falls from mountains to valleys
and the streams moving and swelling toward the seas
I move with my lover
close my eyes
and see again the indigo deeps
Lady of Heaven
I open and embrace the stars

Psyche Lying Awake

In this shuttered palace, neither moon nor torch
has illumined my nights or lit
on the eyes closed now in dreams beside   me,
on the arms that embraced, the pleasuring hands,
and all the rest—all the rest that my body,
visionary of touch, uses to paint its portraits.
The veil of night still hides his face,
and though my fingertips have traced it,
the thought that in daylight I might see
and not know it—that thought
robs me of contentment.

The days have become less and less to me,
uninhabited days with their fine empty rooms
and their unpeopled gardens, nothing
so worth seeing as the secret face of night—
my spirit yearns for that alone.
I will wake with bats and owls now,
and leave the day to brighter creatures.
What monster have I taken to myself,
with nothing left for me but darkness?
If I had a lamp, what I would not give
for one moment in the light.

Hymn to Bacchus

O Bacchus, Liber, liberator
I drink from your cup and restraints fall away
Poetry waterfalls from my lips
and kisses too—I give myself over
myself to myself, myself to life
myself to you—only in you
have I found freedom, O lord of the vine.

> The grape devoured, the seed cast out
> seeks its source, and earth returns it
> from grave to life, a new vine climbing
> twining and bringing forth both fruit
> and the spiral tendrils of recollection.

O Bacchus, Liber, awakener
I am your mother, your spouse, yourself.
The cup I drink from, the cup you offer
overflows my soul's most secret well.

Mother of Shadows

I. Persephone at the Cleft Stone

All days were flowering then
and redolent of Mother's love
every step brushed by the weaving grass
and blessed by the moist black soil
The clouds in the sky were things of beauty
and never covered the sun except
to water the thirsty acres of wheat
the wild wheat spilling over
the shoulders of the land
All days were bright and pleasant then
and I expected no change
never expected, never
the voices from the rock

At the edge of the flowery meadow
gray stone thrusting up through the blooms
hiding the sun as I drew closer
following a butterfly to red flowers
that grew right out of a great black
cleft in the stone
I reached for them
simple and greedy
the air at the crevice
cold, cold and still
then suddenly rushing with a rising shriek
then battering like the surf
with a million voices, a million wails
of loss, pain, unnamable sorrow
confusion, loneliness, desire

I pressed myself against the stone
watched twilight shadow the meadow
tried not to hear

But when the threnody had trailed
into silence, the silence
was worse
I forced my ear to the cleft
and listened
far, far below
a single choked sob

Crickets in the meadow
evening blooms releasing scent
Mother waiting at home
believing me still innocent
a single choked sob
a black crack in the rock
I squeezed through

II. PERSEPHONE AMONG THE DEAD

Deeper than dreams
down, far down
beneath the flowery earth
I came to the land of shadows
and the shadows moved
but were without life
and their eyes stared at me
empty and full of
all they had forgotten
and the endless mourning
for something they might have loved

They begged me to weep with them
and held out their red fruit to me
said, Eat
eat and know what we know

the unnameable sorrow
I took the red fruit
It glowed like fire against the shades
I ate the red seeds
though I feared what might take root
said to myself
I am alive
made myself believe it

I thought of babes I had seen
newborns wretchedly sobbing
without power to do more
outraged at their confinement
in small helplessness
I thought of a mother's patient arms
strong hopeful arms
carrying her baby back and forth
back and forth
gently dancing the newborn
full into the world
I knew the unnameable sorrow

and I knew the unnameable joy
I became mother of shadows

To the Cauldron Tender

Moonwise she has gathered the herbs,
Left them to steep in water from the pure source—
Now, little one, it is up to you
To tend the fire,
To stir the cauldron
A year and a day while she watches,
Ceaseless and vigilant
Lest the fire die, the roiling water calm,
And all be lost and left to do again.

In that black womb,
Dross distills:
Three precious drops
To be caught quickly.

Put your moistened thumb to your mouth
And taste wisdom if you dare—
For you will awaken and know no rest.
She will pursue you through the elements,
Faster than a greyhound after a hare,
Until you are nothing left but a seed
Helpless upon the threshing floor
Scratched by her hen feet,
Picked clean by her black beak
Gaping open at last
To swallow you whole.

There is no other way than to go
Headfirst down into that dark maw;
Embrace your engulfment, or be
Stillborn, never to know
The fair river that will carry you home.

Her Horse

She's upon me
She rides me
Her spurs flame at my sides
I cannot see my hooves
that thunder her rhythm
but she guides them unerring

I could shake off
her quicksilver bridle
but this is the hunt
that I too love
Let her jump me
however she will

Tuxedo Cat's Haiku

I.

Evil chipmunk taunts,
"Chirp, chirp!" He scurries away—
The other side of the fence.

II.

Lizard, you are mine.
I stalk, I pounce—oh, bother!
Detachable tail.

Two Dreams

I must have known you before

Looking for her
I went into a church
dark
mumbled words holding secrets from me
A priest went into the confessional

I know those eyes

shadows clinging deep in the corners
unpierced by candles flickering
a few old women and me alone
and the priest shuttered in
waiting to hear
curtains waving

Even the moment we open our eyes
say hello
one of us is receding

Why did I climb all those steps?
not even a statue
strange church
crimson hangings
congregation of ghosts

I must have known you before
thousands of years ago
maybe

Not here
not what I came for
I should have known

I dreamed
time is one
old fear
new love

The Blasted Tower

After so many clouded years
and the air heavy with his lies,
the women's words finally spark the storm,
the lightning strike in the night
that means she can never go back—
revelation and destruction in the same moment.
Laughing in the ruin
with the brands still falling around her
at last she knows
she really did hear, all that time,
the thunder drumming—
not, as he told her,
planes rumbling toward the airport,
distantly passing trains, whatever else
he could conjure to make delusion of her truth.
And now she knows that when
the tower is leveled, she
alone and tall on the plain,
will draw the lightning
and grasp the jagged bolt,
wield it,
and live.

Witch's Waking

After they made love, her husband fell
asleep, but she lay with her back to him
and gazed into the lingering fire until
she saw the shape of things,
and heard the fire sing, *The spark
will catch, the spark at heart,
where the seed is; feed it, feed it,
give it air.* She breathed. She saw
her feet among the coals; flame
licked from her mouth. She saw
her husband didn't know her, saw
their hearts burned differently.
Lonely, dark, and cold without me,
sang the fire, *you cannot hold me.*
She knew the dragon in its lair. She
remembered what to do: a heather broom
took her place, and up the chimney,
like a spark, she flew away, across the moon.

> *Lonely and dark without me,*
> *merry and bright my flame.*
> *But you can never hold me;*
> *you can never be the same.*
> *If you look into the mirror,*
> *if you peer in through the cracks,*
> *if you see with open heart,*
> *then you never will go back.*

Becoming

I am a snake
      shedding skin
I am the moon
      wax and wane
I am the tide
      out and in
I am a woman becoming

Free like the bird
      taking flight
Strong like the tree
      leaf and root
I hear the song
      of the night
I am a woman becoming

POMEGRANATE

I sit with my half
perfect in my hands
cupped as if they had been formed
long ago to be filled
with this beckoning redness
       like holding my own heart
       a cutaway view of the chambers
The fruit flesh pulses
bleeding juice through my fingers
staining my thighs
       A voice whispers
       communion
       in my ear
       Come, union
       I whisper in my heart
On a gentler day
I would pluck the seeds out
one by one with careful fingertips
Tonight I raise the fruit
to my lips like a chalice

Priestess Song

I have been a storm on the beach
and foam on the sea
I have been a teacher of birds
and crossed the distances
I have tended the fire
of nineteen maidens
I have spun the distaff
and danced the wheel
I have poured out my waters
and given milk from my breasts
I have walked the moon's path
over the waves
I have healed the scars
of the Bridge of Swords
I have mended the words
and given them life

I am a candle in the shadows
I am a thread through the labyrinth
I am a flute that sings
with the breath of the Mighty
I am lover and lover
stained with pomegranate
I walk with lions at my side
and call the wilderness
I balance the pillars
I am at the gateway
I see through the mirror
I live

I will make the voyage
to the veil's lifting
I will bring back apples
from the Land of the Young

Part Two

TURNINGS

Women and men are the wheels of the world.

—Robin Williamson
"Lammas"

BEHIND THE DOOR

Hidden
in that darkness deep as the night of oceans,
behind the door that
opens and closes to its own
heedless rhythm—
I know how you wait,
yearning for your gateway
to these skies and forests,
streets and fields of trial
and transformation.
You will make
a bloody entrance,
and bind me faster
than any golden band.

With back and shoulders and braced arms—
small might—
I push
closed against you.
But you
are uncontained and strong, and
the smallest gap is enough
for the breath of your desire:
no more is needed to fan spark to flame,
melting will—
not such a great task after all.

I too have been waiting,
moon by moon,
marking the time with blood,
ebbing and flowing in spirals
toward you.
My dreams of you
are pegged by stars to the arching sky.

Late-January Roses

Under a clouded sky, almost alone,
I walked among the winter roses in
the garden by the river, all at home
with brown, dead-looking, naked canes that reached
out thorns to snag me to their tended mounds.
They caught my skirt, and so I bent, and pricked
My finger carelessly. The blood, I found,
awakened me, and cleared my sight. I saw
that green showed through upon those canes. I saw
the small red buds where fresher stems would spring.
Beneath my feet I felt the coming thaw
rising from the heart of Earth. I knew,
almost, my portent from the roses then:
new life was stirring in my belly, too.

IN THE BELLY

In the embrace of the salt sea
floating is easy, waves
are lost memories
and the comfort of the present.
The spark upon the water,
the flaring sea-fire foretells
the beacon's summoning.
For now the pull of the moon
and navigation by starlight
are enough, and soon enough
will set me on the shore
of my new land.

UNDER THIS WARMING SUN

Sitting, musing under this warming sun—
So like a lover's touch, light on my cheek—
Dark eyes and moonlight still possess my sight;
The voice of night and dream of passion seek
To captivate my other senses and
Enfold me in their silence. At the peak
Of love, of starry vision, the embrace
Consumes desire, and leaves no way to speak.

There is a tune for what I cannot sing,
Heard in the whispering of the winter trees
That stand on darkened paths; but this is spring—
Dark eyes and love fade with the growing light:
Too gladly would I give in to the dream
And the seduction of enshrouding night.

SACRAMENT

At first
you looked like a stranger
Then I knew
with the sureness of sensation
You are my prodigal
returning to fields
long abandoned
but waiting
for the crackle
of lightning to ground
herald of the rains
and the tree rooted so deep that
the earth
has no boundary

Lightning strikes and I
explode with your beauty
When the rains are over
all is melted
into greenery

I understand Spring

Rite of Spring

(written after seeing the Joffrey's reconstruction of Diaghilev's ballet)

chosen, shaking
first steps quivering
look the sun in the eye
begin my dance
the Bearskins close by
watching with all of them
waiting
I think I will never move again
after this
flying fast for them
watching
for me
slow
each movement
stretch of my arms
toward the sun
stamp of my foot
on the sod
laborious
as though I watch myself
through muddied water
of spring streams
fierce and full down the mountain
not even reflecting
the sun I dance to
until
wracked with dancing
I drop and become
earth
their earth
wed with the sun

TO DEBORAH ON THE FIRST DAY OF SPRING

Today I wore for the first time the dress
you gave me from your hippie past. It reached
my ankles, tickled my palms with lace,
and from its twirl and swish I quick beseeched
assurance of some sure return to grace,
to childlike selflessness and joy in each
new moment's life—the existential yes
of flowing water, trees in bud, the breach
from underworld to shining air of seeds
and souls alike—all that we call this day
Persephone. And when I danced in your
blue-flowered dress and watched my child at play
down by the waterfall, I knew once more
that in my reach were all my spirit's needs.

Spring Equinox

Now springes the spray.
All for love ich am so seeke
That slepen I ne may.
      —Middle English lyric

Reeling on the precipice of night and day,
a sword edge,
I find myself acute in my imbalance—
like the medieval lyricists
epidemically out of sync with
the turning wheel of the seasons.
We feel most strange when the world
is blossoming and we
remain tight shut against life.

They put it all down to lovesickness,
those troubadours and minnesingers—
desire unfulfilled. We
have no desire, or desire
nothing of worth, or
don't know what we desire....
I can only speak for myself.

I have been waiting
for some Orphic hand to lead me
out and away from the dead land.
But I see
in the now-even light
that I carry the darkness with me
and it is only I
who have made it lifeless.

Anniversary, April 1

Most look upon this day as April Fools':
a time of playing with accepted rules,
of slapstick pranks, trickery, and jokes—
but you and I, my love, are not most folks.
Convenience—little more—led us to choose
this laughing day for solemn vows. And who's
unable to resist the chance to gibe
us for our foolishness as we imbibe
our yearly toast? Not I. We might as well
have married wearing motley, cap, and bells
as we rushed in with trust in love alone.
Now years have passed, and we have wiser grown—
enough that loving has remained our will,
so we two grateful fools are married still.

April Insomnia

As I pace, they inhabit the edges of my sight:
cats stalking shadowly in and out of moonlight
filtered through curtains in the unsleeping house,
in the unstill night, when the carouse
of whip-poor-wills and the year's first spring
peepers unsettle every worn-out thing
still unused to open windows at night.

The cats enjoy their nocturnal prowl,
serenely undisturbed by woodland owl
calls in the wild outside night.
Their feline souls take pure, alert delight
in padding through the moon-transformed terrain
of their own interior domain.
But the dog, alone asleep, dreams and howls.

BELTANE

The birth night of the radiant brow,
of the golden-haired boy and
the miraculous colt, the gestation
of the cut grain complete—now is time
to light the hilltop fires that call
the sun to bless the blossoming land,
the fires that call back the lost
and wandering hearts, the fires
that halo lovers' holy bowers.
We have such faith in the fire
of love to catch and spread and blaze
beauty around our Earth.
     When morning
comes, dew-washed and garlanded, we feel
in our bones the fire-heated, sun-heated
seed crowning out of the soil
and we breathe and we cry out
"Unite!" for the newborn of the Mother
sustains us, as she does, as we—
in our love, in our dance—nurture
Earth and seed: the great returning.
We ribbon the Maypole to turn
the Wheel and ourselves become
the Earth-rooted, sky-rooted,
fire-reaching, sun-reaching, uniting Tree.
We have such faith in our love.

SUMMERLAND

It is here in the ripening corn
and in the grass under our bare toes.
The pecans forming at the ends
of their branches are bursting with it.
The crickets thrum to its nearness,
and a butterfly lifts its veil.

I see it in your eyes, the color
of the distant and changing sea,
and in the perpetual motion of our son—
leaving his apple for the birds,
he calls, "I'm going to visit the trees!"

The breeze from the garden stirs
our memories, and the westering sun
does not let us forget as we kiss,
then follow after our boy.

The Corn

Hand in hand with the harvest:
the winnowing, the knowing
what is needed, what is not.

Broken from the stalk, the ear
is stripped, the naked kernels
a common revelation.

We split, bend, braid the husks, shape
a rough, hollow human form—
destined for the pyre. The seed

roots its life in our bellies.
With thankful lips we pass our
common cup from hand to hand.

In the Fallow Garden

Regrets embed themselves
into a November twilight
as I take clothes off the line
pin by pin, deliberate.
A noisy arrow of geese
calls my sight upward;
their passing draws away
a dusty curtain.
The wind plays a rattle of leaves;
the sky promises stars.
I remember falling in love,
and understand its limit.

A Dream I Had While Nursing My Son on Thanksgiving Morning

It seems there was a war or something,
so my cousin and I left
our gathered family, went to fight,
and we were wounded—maybe killed.

I lost sight of him and went
on alone, until I saw
among the ruins, standing tall
and gowned in starry clouds, the queen of all.
I knew her when she smiled and called.
She knelt, and I lay down my head
and in her lap I rested till
she helped me up and pointed to
a line of whispering trees. I knew,
I knew what lay beyond them: soft
green hills and scented grass—
I had been there in my dreams
when I still lived.

So to the hills I went again
and met my cousin on the road.
I grabbed him by the arm and said,
"I have to talk with you about this now,
before we both go back." He led
me to the beach, and by the endless surf
we told each other where we'd been.
Our eyes met then,
and I had barely time to say "I love you"—
I perched him on my hip, a smaller him,
and bore him back to that family gathering.

My grandma took him in her arms,
and as he lay there in her lap,
I talked to him as though he were
a little baby. But a moment came
when I felt wide awake, and I
remembered who he was and what
we'd said and what we'd shared there
on the beach. I tried to speak that way
to him again. But he was just a babe,
and I was still asleep.

THE LAST NIGHT OF NOVEMBER

The leafless trees somehow change
the color of the night
and the look of the moon.
Their skeleton dance in the wind,
the empty nut hulls clinging,
the unconcealed nests
vulnerable in the branches—
all clamor death.
Yet it's not foreboding
on the face of the moon,
but clarity, and the sky
is implacably serene.

BLACKBIRDS

From fall to spring on any day,
through any window, I might glance
and see the yard an iridescent sea
of blackbirds—red-winged, starlings, all varieties.

They are sensitive to sound and shadow:
I keep my distance from the windows—
go too near, or open one,
and up they rise in gleaming waves

that bathe the sky before they sweep
onto the shores of other lawns—
ours is just one seed-rich piece
of their unbounded winter country.

Winter Seed

Oh, warm,
warm and silent and blanketed
I sleep,
curled tight around my tenderness,
giving no more tears to loss—
the time
for that is past, the time
of the dying blooms. Now
alone in the dark, sorrow
is less than a memory.
My eyes, closed,
dance dreams of beauty to come.
When the sun
kisses me awake again,
I will grow them true.

"If We Don't Turn the Wheel, It Will Not Turn"

Our ancestors in their simplicity,
we hear, believed the spent midwinter sun
would die at last and never rise again
without their rites—so every turning of
the seasons had its keeping and its forms,
and failure in them meant the end of all.
"Now we know better"—or do we know less?
In the pattern's loss, what have we gained?
The days we set aside to mourn the sun
or drive the cattle through the fires or bless
the fields joined our spirits, bodies, minds
to the moving heart of all. We did not turn
the earth upon its axis—what we turned,
and still might turn, was purely our own souls.

Part Three

WATER AND OTHER ELEMENTS

For the elemental creatures go
About my table to and fro

—William Butler Yeats
"To Ireland in the Coming Times"

OVER THE WATER

Over the water, you are waking,
but I will soon lay down my pen and sleep;
while I rest, you will cross to the isles,
and in the waves that spark and leap,
you may see shadows of old smiles
that know our hearts' partaking
of shared and partnered dreams—
only the ocean lies between.

Invitation

She sends her call
soft kiss on the breeze
blowing down
from the mountains
scent beckoning
from the mountains
drawing you on
promise of sticky sweetness
drawing you on
to some wild orchard where trees
blossom and green and offer their fruit
all at a time
offering fruit
to waiting desire
bending down branches
to answer your thirst
knowing your hunger
bending down branches
You
have been to this place
before
barefoot on the green
juice on your chin
in some wild orchard
where every breathless breath invites you
back

The Man from the Sea

My lover looked at me with other eyes,
and in my arms I held the wild
and surging sea, and felt the breathing waves
beneath my legs...

                        my coracle
low in the water, sinking still,
but this time fearless of the boned
imprisonment told for the journey's end,
for at my side the man of changes swam.
My skin and bones, my coracle—
I knew and left the fortress holding me
the moment that I took the hand
he offered and the water closed above.
I breathed with ease now in his ebb and flow
and blithely followed deeper where he led.
The tower of bones in which he tested me
I found was nothing but the hall
of my own hundred selves. Without my boat,
free to ride his horses at his side
across his salty pastures, I could laugh
at who I'd been—

                       laugh and forgive, and plan
for love's return upon the farther shore.

In the Circle

In candle glow and incense smoke I heard
Your breath as waves that sing upon the shore,
Yet hold the promise of the tempest's roar;
And when you spoke, there something in me stirred—
The water's voice, that called its hidden word
And made me shiver, wet me to the core,
Yet drew me on until I knew no more,
But floated in a realm where gray eyes lured
Me to the arms of love, and there I found
My senses filling with the rising tide
Of laughter and the joy of dreams unbound,
For all time freed from inhibition's grip;
And dancing with the waves and wind allied,
I surfaced, tasting salt upon my lip.

To My Love Asleep

Sometimes when I come late to bed I lie
awake until a passing headlight beams
in through the blinds and shows your dreaming eyes.
Then I might wonder what unconscious streams
your night-loosed mind and soul are sailing on,
what sights appear upon the shores, and in
your secret ship what forms you don.
I wonder, would I know you for my kin
and you know me if I could somehow drift
myself into your dreams, or is the rift
of daily separate ways too great to span
in simple sleep—but what in dreaming can
not be attempted? Steering by desire,
I sail to meet you at the beacon's fire.

THE NET

In the waves together
the double drumming of heartbeats
becomes the sound in a shell
the tides of our blood joined
with the pulse of the sea
Flesh becomes permeable
silver mesh
a net
I am caught up and
the waters pass through
I am breathing in water
swimming with you
in the water
suspended
embraced
flowing
with the power of water
I am not eyes or ears or mouth
or flesh at all
I am just the flowing
and you are the flowing
and we pass through the net
together

The Shore

I am the soft sand
washed over by your ocean
formed and reformed with every
pull of the moon threading
silver through her dark web

Quiet
patient
I listen and wait
breathe and sigh in rhythm
swallow salt
become salt
I am gritty with it

You bring me
drifting from undreamt horizons
shining bits of treasure
lives long gone
swallowed and disgorged
becoming me until
I piece by piece return

I am the soft sand
washed over by your ocean
every impression lost to
the turning tides
and I myself
am worn away

A MEDITATION

And at the end of this
round of desire, what then?
Does attainment stop
the Wheel's turning, or
does it slip from the hand
as soon as grasped
to start desire rolling again
along an endless-sighted path?
What matters besides hope,
the horizon's glimmer,
the resurgence of life?

SPIDER

Old woman,
I see your tapestries everywhere—
branches, railings, high corners—
and there you are, waiting—
mending and tending—waiting,
like me, for something to come
(innocent and sustaining)—
meanwhile mending and tending,
spinning out what I can
from what I have,
what I am.

Call to the Darkness

In the forest of the night-roaming hunters,
where moonlight through leaves dapples your skin
so that you too may fade into verdure,
choose the darker path, or no path at all.
Tread softly through the bracken
as though you walk on beast feet
that know well this meeting-ground
of growth and decay,
where moving shadows draw you deeper
to make you one of them among the trees
that, whispering, answer the endless hum
of the small and hidden ones of the branches.
Look through your night eyes, shed your skin;
find your own voice to call to the darkness—
and dance.
There will be nothing human
in the forest of the night-roaming hunters.

Meeting

I hear your call
bellow in the forest
rising from the depths to the
rhythm of hooves
on rain-packed, leaf-matted
soil
flesh
I answer
changing too
as I make my way
to the clearing
where moonlight
catches beckoning eyes
seeking eyes
drawing together
as I call you by your other name

And afterward my fingers
twine in your hair
searching for antlers

RECONCILIATION

In a dream
or another life
we met between the fires,
flames casting red gold around us
like something lanterned within
shining out to touch
each other and the night's
brushwork of drumbeats
and voices. We stood
in the center of our own making,
the shadows sliding away.

Your hands
made a prayer around my face.
Our lips spoke their joined language
of sweet flesh and shared breath,
saying, The past has died
and I yearn no more.

Boy Playing

A whole world evolves in the living room:
Cardboard bricks are streets and railroad tracks,
leading from the fire station to the farm.
The hospital perches high on the couch;
dogs sleep in the attic of the yellow house
in the corner by the gas station, next to the airport.
This world is populated with vehicles: tow trucks,
tractors, pickups, police cars, a school bus,
ambulance, bulldozer, and of course fire trucks.
Here in this world a three-year-old boy
is creator, preserver, destroyer, creator again.
The one law is movement.

Traveling to Florida

We get into the car early, let my father drive,
doze, and wake up where the land has changed:
it is flat, flat, with row upon row
of pecan trees full-leafed beside the road—
as though the seasons have moved on
since the morning, when our mountain
buckeyes, hickories, dogwoods, and beeches
were just beginning to stir,
and instead of our red oak and white oak,
soon there is live oak,
moss-hung, hundred years old,
hunkering on the verges. We cross
the state line and stop for lunch,
my son marveling out the window:
"I've never seen a palm tree in my life—
but here I'm looking at a whole line of them!"
After we resume the road,
the arborial world transforms again:
everywhere, everywhere orange trees—
so improbable, so April-early
drooping with such wide-awake fruit.

Venetian Glass

Pink-arched, dappled city
I know from books, paintings,
movies only, and may never see
except through lampwork trinkets
throwing shadows
I will become a collector
I want
the jewel colors
the translucence and hidden depths
palatial remnants in the light
lagoon sighs, Bellini splendor,
Titian life
Millefiori, sommerso, cristallo—
incantatory syllables
substance liquid yet solid seeming
like the hidden movement
slow and unseen
behind all things

SUNSET OVER LAKE ONTARIO

We walk over the water-smoothed stones of the beach
to a driftwood log where we sit
and rest our eyes on the shifting sky.
We see the changes as they tableau before us,
but not the actual changing—not
the occult process that streaks and swirls
fiery unnamed shades of yellow, red, pink, orange
over the restless waters.

Without speaking, we promise not to speak
in the presence of what we cannot describe.
We would drink it all down if we could,
or breathe it through every pore.

We try not to stare at the closing eye
of the day, but its burning red-orange
is a seduction—we could look at it long
and see it ever after. We resist temptation
and at last are reprieved by the blessed dusk,
the between time before the stars, when the earth
undergoes its own dark changes, shadows
lending shape to elemental creatures
at the water's edge, at the fringes
of our sight—we acknowledge them
without voice or conscious thought . . .
and know it is time to leave.
Walking through the white sweet clover to the road,
we savor what we have tasted—
our world transfigured, transformations far beyond
our human reach, yet reaching us—and wonder
what we would be if we closed all our days
silently watching the sky into night.

About the Author

Kathryn Hinds grew up near Rochester, NY, then moved to New York City to attend Barnard College and the Graduate Center of the City University of New York. She now lives in the beautiful mountains of north Georgia, but migrates back to the southern shore of Lake Ontario nearly every summer. Although Kathryn has held a variety of jobs—waitress, administrative assistant, early childhood educator, research assistant, editorial assistant, French and Latin tutor, library information specialist—writing has been her constant occupation. Her published works include poetry, short stories, a coauthored book on Celtic mythology, and more than fifty nonfiction books for children and young adults. Kathryn has also worked as a freelance editor since 1991 and an English instructor at the University of North Georgia since 2011, and she sometimes moonlights as a belly dancer. Her main job, however—according to certain members of her household—is to ensure that cat food is available on demand.

Made in the USA
Charleston, SC
05 June 2013